UNUSUAL LiFe CYCLES OF

INVERTEBRATES

by Jaclyn Jaycox

CAPSTONE PRESS
a capstone imprint

Capstone Captivate is published by Capstone Press, an imprint of Capstone.
1710 Roe Crest Drive
North Mankato, Minnesota 56003
www.capstonepub.com

Library of Congress Cataloging-in-Publication Data
Names: Jaycox, Jaclyn, 1983- author.
Title: Unusual life cycles of birds / Jaclyn Jaycox.
Description: North Mankato, Minnesota : Pebble, an imprint of Capstone, [2021] | Series: Unusual life cycles | Includes bibliographical references and index. | Audience: Ages 8-11 | Audience: Grades 4-6 | Summary: "Have you ever heard of a bird that lays its eggs on the ground instead of in a nest? What about a bird that lays eggs in other birds' nests? Young readers will learn all about killdeers, cuckoo birds, and other birds with unusual life cycles"-- Provided by publisher. Identifiers: LCCN 2021002871 (print) | LCCN 2021002872 (ebook) | ISBN 9781496695574 (hardcover) | ISBN 9781496697011 (paperback) | ISBN 9781977155221 (pdf) | ISBN 9781977156846 (kindle edition) Subjects: LCSH: Birds--Life cycles--Juvenile literature. | Birds--Miscellanea--Juvenile literature. Classification: LCC QL676.2 .J39 2021 (print) | LCC QL676.2 (ebook) | DDC 598.156--dc23
LC record available at https://lccn.loc.gov/2021002871
LC ebook record available at https://lccn.loc.gov/2021002872

Image Credits
Minden Pictures: Fred Bavendam, 15, Norburt Wu, 17, Piotr Naskrecki, 29; Newscom/Paulo de Oliveria/NHPA/Avalon.red, 19; Science Source/ Tom McHugh, 21; Shutterstock: Achkin, 11, D. Kucharski K. Kurcharska, 23, Gerry Bishop, 13, Johan Larson, 5, Kim Howell, 7, Laky_981, 9, Meister Photos, 27, Mirek Kijewski, cover, Nik Bruining, 25

Design elements: Shutterstock: emEF, Max Krasnov

Editorial Credits
Editor: Gena Chester; Designer: Bobbie Nuytten; Media Researcher: Kelly Garvin; Production Specialist: Laura Manthe

All internet sites appearing in back matter were available and accurate when this book was sent to press.

Words in **bold** are in the glossary.

Table of Contents

CHAPTER 1

Invertebrate Life Cycle

A colorful butterfly flutters in the air. Can you believe these beautiful creatures aren't even born with wings? Butterflies belong to a group of animals called invertebrates. These animals do not have backbones. There are over 1 million different animals in this group. In fact, invertebrates make up more than 90 percent of all animals in the world.

Invertebrates go through life cycles called **metamorphosis**. Metamorphosis is a series of changes that happens as they grow. There are four stages in an invertebrate's life. Let's look at the life cycle of a butterfly.

A Cairns birdwing butterfly

A butterfly starts as an egg. A caterpillar hatches from the egg. This is the **larval** stage. Caterpillars spend most of their time eating and growing. When the caterpillar is fully grown, it becomes a **pupa**. It forms a hard shell around itself. The shell protects the pupa from **predators** and harsh weather. The pupa spends weeks transforming inside this shell. Then, out pops a butterfly! Soon it flies away, ready to find a **mate** to continue the life cycle.

Most invertebrates experience transformations like this. But there are a few that do things a little differently. Some skip one or two of these stages of life. Others spend much of their lives underground. And some rely on other animals in order to complete their life cycles.

BUTTERFLY LIFE CYCLE

caterpillar

pupa

egg

adult butterfly

CHAPTER 2

Skipping Stages

Mayflies

Mayflies go through a life cycle different than butterflies. Their life cycle does not have a pupal stage. It's called incomplete metamorphosis.

Mayflies begin life in the water. Males and females mate above the water. Females lay their eggs on the surface of a lake or river. Both parents die shortly after.

The eggs sink to the bottom. They stick to rocks or plants. Larvae hatch from the eggs. These young mayflies are called **nymphs**. They spend up to two years underwater eating and growing. Then they float up to the surface. They shed their skin, or molt. They are now winged adults.

A pair of mayflies in a river in Hungary

The adult mayflies float on the water's surface while their wings harden. Then they fly away from the water and land on the shore. Although they are adults, they cannot fly very well yet. And they are not ready to mate.

Mayflies go through one more molt. This happens about 24 to 48 hours after they leave the water. They are the only insect that has two winged-adult life stages. After the second molt, they will only live for a very short time. They can't eat or drink in this last stage of life. Some live a few days, but others live only a few hours. Their only goal now is to mate and lay eggs so the life cycle can repeat.

Fact!

Dolania americana is a type of mayfly. The females have the shortest adult lives of any insect. After their last molt, they live less than five minutes.

Mayflies can be anywhere from 0.25 inches (0.6 centimeters) to 1.1 inches (2.8 cm) long.

Cicadas

Cicadas also go through incomplete metamorphosis. They lay eggs in trees. Nymphs hatch from the eggs. They drop to the ground and **burrow** into the soil. They eat sap from tree roots.

Some cicadas live in the nymph stage for up to 17 years. They spend almost their whole lives growing underground. They shed their skin many times.

When cicadas are fully grown, they tunnel to the surface. They do not go through a pupal stage. They climb a nearby tree and shed their skin one more time. They are now winged adults. They take off flying and search for mates. They live up to six weeks as adults.

A cicada digging its way out of the soil

HERCULES BEETLES

Much like cicadas, Hercules beetles live underground for most of their lives. Females lay eggs in the soil. Larvae spend up to two years underground. They turn into pupae and then adults before heading for the surface. They can live up to one year as adults.

Octopuses

Octopuses are another type of invertebrate that skips part of the life cycle. Baby octopuses hatch from eggs. They do not go through a pupal stage. Instead, they look like miniature versions of their parents. The babies grow quickly. After one to two years, the octopuses are adults. They are ready to mate.

Male octopuses die a few months after mating. Females lay the eggs, protect them, and keep them clean. The eggs can take up to 10 months to hatch. The females do not eat during this time. They put all their energy into caring for the eggs. They die when the eggs hatch. The babies are on their own. Only a small number of the baby octopuses survive.

Giant Pacific octopuses hatching

CHAPTER 3

Reverse Life Cycle

Immortal Jellyfish

Immortal jellyfish have a very unique life cycle. Like other invertebrates, they begin as eggs. Larvae hatch from the eggs. The larvae find their way to the ocean floor. They attach themselves to rocks and turn into **polyps**. Polyps look like small tubes. They eat and grow. Eventually, buds grow on the polyps. The buds form into jellyfish and break free. About two to four weeks later, the jellyfish reach the adult stage. They are fully grown and ready to mate.

Immortal jellyfish are able to live forever! If they are hurt or starving, they can change back into polyps. They can do this over and over again instead of dying.

Two immortal jellyfish in their polyp stage of life

CHAPTER 4

Parasites

Parasites live on other plants and animals. The plant or animal the parasite is living on is called a host. Parasites are a type of invertebrate. They rely on their hosts for survival.

Tongue-Eating Louse

The tongue-eating louse is a type of parasite. All tongue-eating lice are born male. Lice swim into the gills of a fish. One of the group will turn into a female. The female then travels into the mouth of the fish. She attaches herself to the fish's tongue. She feeds off blood from the tongue. The female takes so much blood, the tongue dies. Then, the louse takes over and acts as the fish's tongue.

Males stay in the fish's gills. To mate, they travel into the fish's mouth where the female is. Shortly after mating, the female gives birth. The baby lice leave the mouth in search of another host.

A tongue-eating louse acts as the tongue of a yellowtail clownfish.

Unionid Mussels

Unionid mussels live in rivers. They go through a parasitic stage in their life cycles. Females carry eggs that develop into larvae. The larvae attach to the fins or gills of a fish. They stay there for weeks or even months while they transform into adults. Their hosts carry them to different areas of the river. Then the mussels drop off their hosts. They live the rest of their lives on the bottom of the river.

Unionid mussels move very little as adults. They need a healthy **habitat** to be able to live and **reproduce**. If one part of the river becomes unhealthy, the mussels won't survive. Using fish to bring larvae to new places ensures the mussels' survival.

ATTRACTING A HOST

Some types of unionid mussels have flaps that look like small fish. This attracts fish. When a fish bites the flap, the mussel releases the larvae. This way, the larvae don't have to search for a host. This gives the larvae a much higher chance of survival.

A unionid mussel has a siphon that acts as its mouth. The siphon pulls in food from the water current to eat.

Lancet Liver Flukes

Lancet liver flukes spend their whole lives inside other animals. Lancet liver flukes begin life as eggs. Snails eat these eggs. While inside the snail, larvae hatch from the eggs. The snail creates a slime ball around them. After about four months, the snail gets rid of the slime and larvae. Ants eat the slime balls and the larvae.

The larvae grow while inside the ant. Some make their way to the ant's brain. If an ant is eaten by a grazing animal like a cow or goat, the larvae survive. They turn into adults inside this third, final host. There, the lancet liver flukes lay eggs. The eggs are passed by the animal. A snail will come to eat the poop with the eggs hiding inside. The life cycle starts all over again.

Lancet liver flukes are so small you need microscopes to see them.

Parasitic Wasps

Parasitic wasps aren't like most types of wasps. They are small and spend much of their lives on or inside another insect. Some types of parasitic wasps mate. But some females are able to reproduce without mating. They find a host in which to lay their eggs. These hosts are usually other insects.

Parasitic wasps have a long stinger-like part. They use it to lay their eggs inside a host. When the larvae hatch, they feed off of the host. The larvae must be careful not to feed so much it kills the host. As long as the host is alive, it gives the larvae a safe place to grow. Some break free from their host when they are ready for the pupal stage. Others go through the pupal stage inside their host.

Two parasitic wasps hatching from their eggs

One type of parasitic wasp uses caterpillar hosts. The larvae grow inside the caterpillar. Then they break through the host's skin. The caterpillar survives and helps the larvae start the pupal stage. It helps the wasps spin their **cocoons**.

The caterpillar spends all its time watching over the cocoons. It fights off predators. It doesn't eat. Adult parasitic wasps come out of the cocoons. The caterpillar dies of starvation. The wasps fly away to find new hosts to continue the life cycle.

Parasitic wasp cocoons on the back of a tobacco hornworm

CHAPTER 5

Protective Mothers

Goliath Bird–Eating Spiders

Goliath bird-eating spiders are a type of tarantula. They are huge! But they start out life as small eggs. A female lays eggs in a web. Then she wraps them up and puts them in a burrow. She guards the eggs. Unlike other kinds of tarantulas, she will even carry the egg sac with her if she needs to leave.

After hatching, the baby spiders stay in the burrow. They do not come out until after they molt for the first time. The spiders molt up to six times in their first year. After two to three years, they are adults. Males die a few months after mating. But females can live up to 20 years in the wild.

Fact!

Goliath bird-eating spiders are the largest tarantulas in the world. Fully grown, they can reach the size of a small puppy.

A goliath bird-eating spider

Glossary

burrow (BUR-oh)—a hole or tunnel used as a home

cocoon (kuh-KOON)—a covering made of silky threads; some insects make a cocoon to protect themselves while changing from larvae to pupae

habitat (HAB-uh-tat)—the home of a plant or animal

larva (LAR-vuh)—an animal at the stage of development between an egg and an adult; larvae is plural for larva

mate (MATE)—to join with another to produce young

metamorphosis (meht-uh-MOR-fuh-siss)—the series of changes some animals go through as they develop from eggs to adults

nymph (NIMF)—a young insect; nymphs change into adults by shedding their skin many times

parasite (PAIR-uh-site)—an animal that lives on or inside another animal or plant and causes harm

polyp (POL-lip)—a small sea animal with a tubular body and a round mouth surrounded by tentacles

predator (PRED-uh-tur)—an animal that hunts other animals for food

pupa (PYOO-pa)—a hard casing with an animal inside

reproduce (ree-pruh-DOOSE)—to breed and have offspring

Read More

Allan, John. *Creepy Crawlies*. Minneapolis: Lerner Publishing, 2019.

Amstutz, Lisa J. *Investigating Animal Life Cycles*. Minneapolis: Lerner Publications, 2015.

Axelrod-Contrada, Joan. *Body Snatchers: Flies, Wasps, and Other Creepy Crawly Zombie Makers*. North Mankato, MN: Capstone Press, 2017.

Internet Sites

Britannica Kids: Invertebrate
kids.britannica.com/students/article/invertebrate/275081

Kiddle: Mayfly Facts for Kids
kids.kiddle.co/Mayfly

National Geographic Kids: Invertebrates
kids.nationalgeographic.com/animals/invertebrates/

Index